Hear!

Ruth Thomson

Photographs by Peter Millard

Contents

Watts Books

London • New York • Sydney

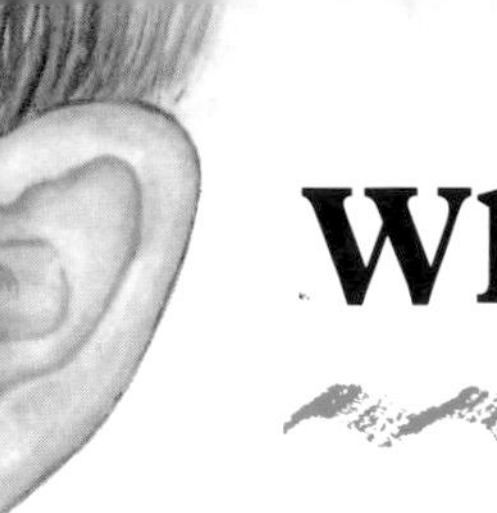

What big ears!

Ears are sound collectors.
The folds channel sounds
down a tube inside your skull.

A sheet of skin, called the eardrum,
stretches across the end of the tube.
It moves to and fro when sounds hit it.
These rapid movements are called vibrations.
The vibrations pass from the eardrum
along three tiny bones to the inner ear.

In the inner ear is a coiled tube.
The sounds are turned
into electrical signals.
The signals go
to your brain,
which sorts out
what each sound is.

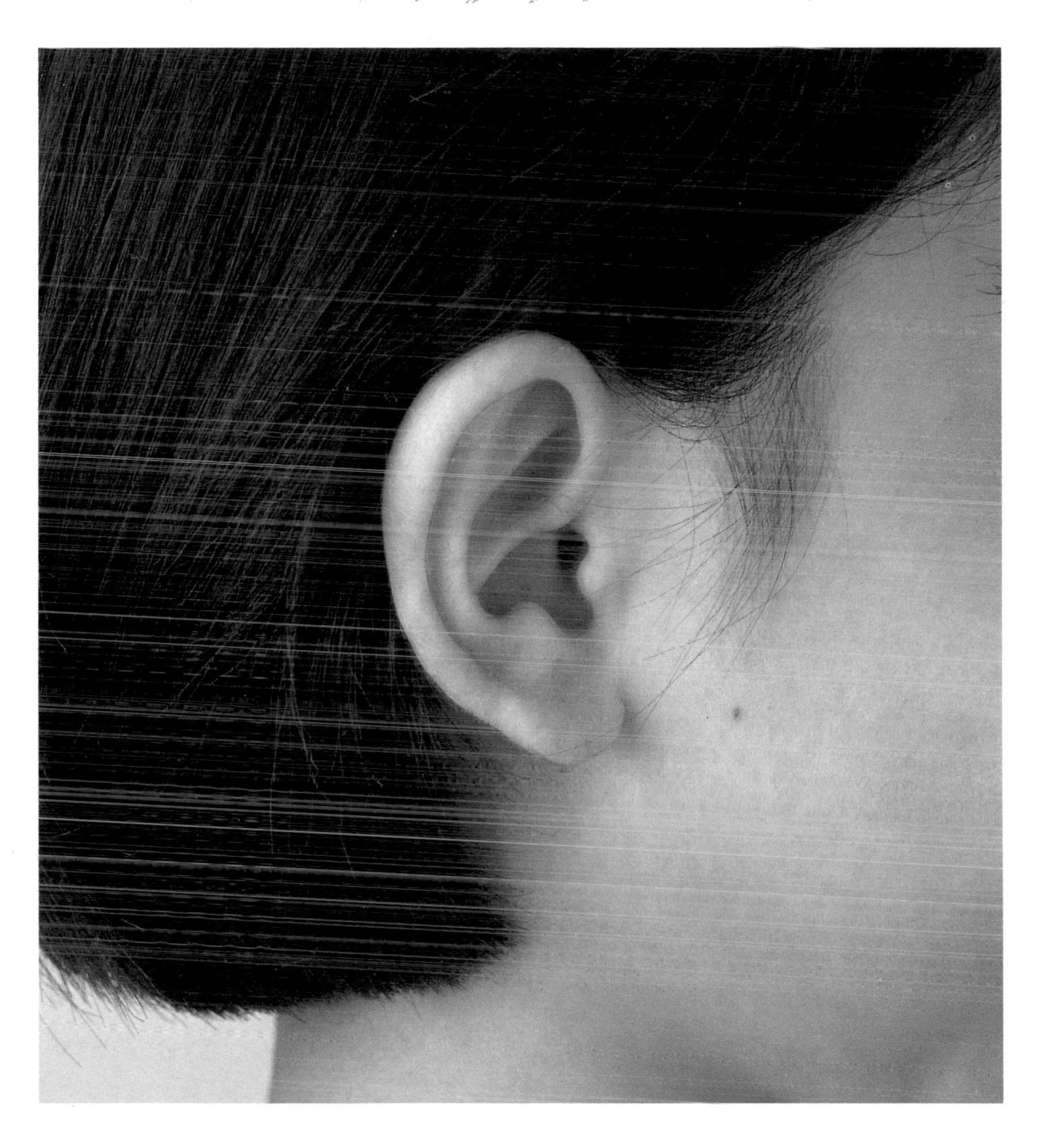

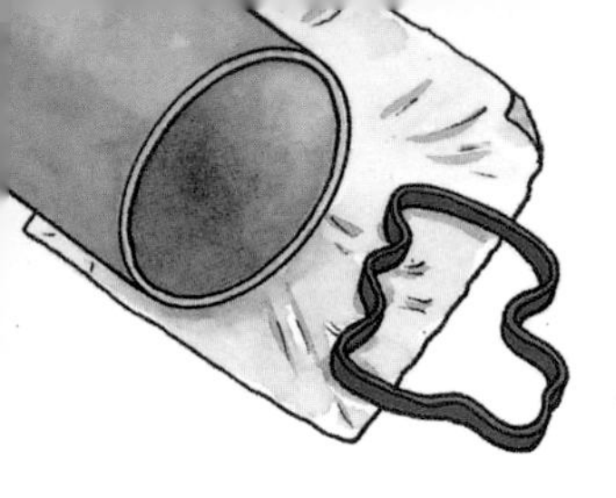

How do you hear?

Get ready

✔Cardboard tube ✔Tissue paper
✔Rubber band

...Get set

Fix a piece of tissue paper over one end of the tube with a rubber band.
Put a finger lightly on the tissue paper.
Speak down the other end of the tube.

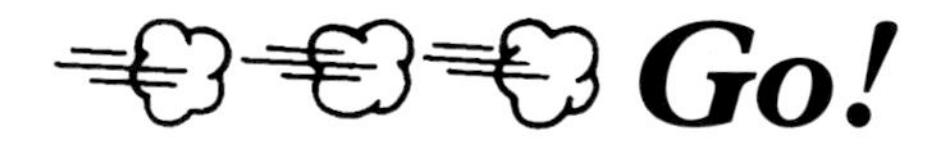

Go!

What can you see? What can you hear?

When things vibrate, they make a sound.
The sound squashes and stretches the air.
You cannot see sound, but you can often see and feel the vibrations.

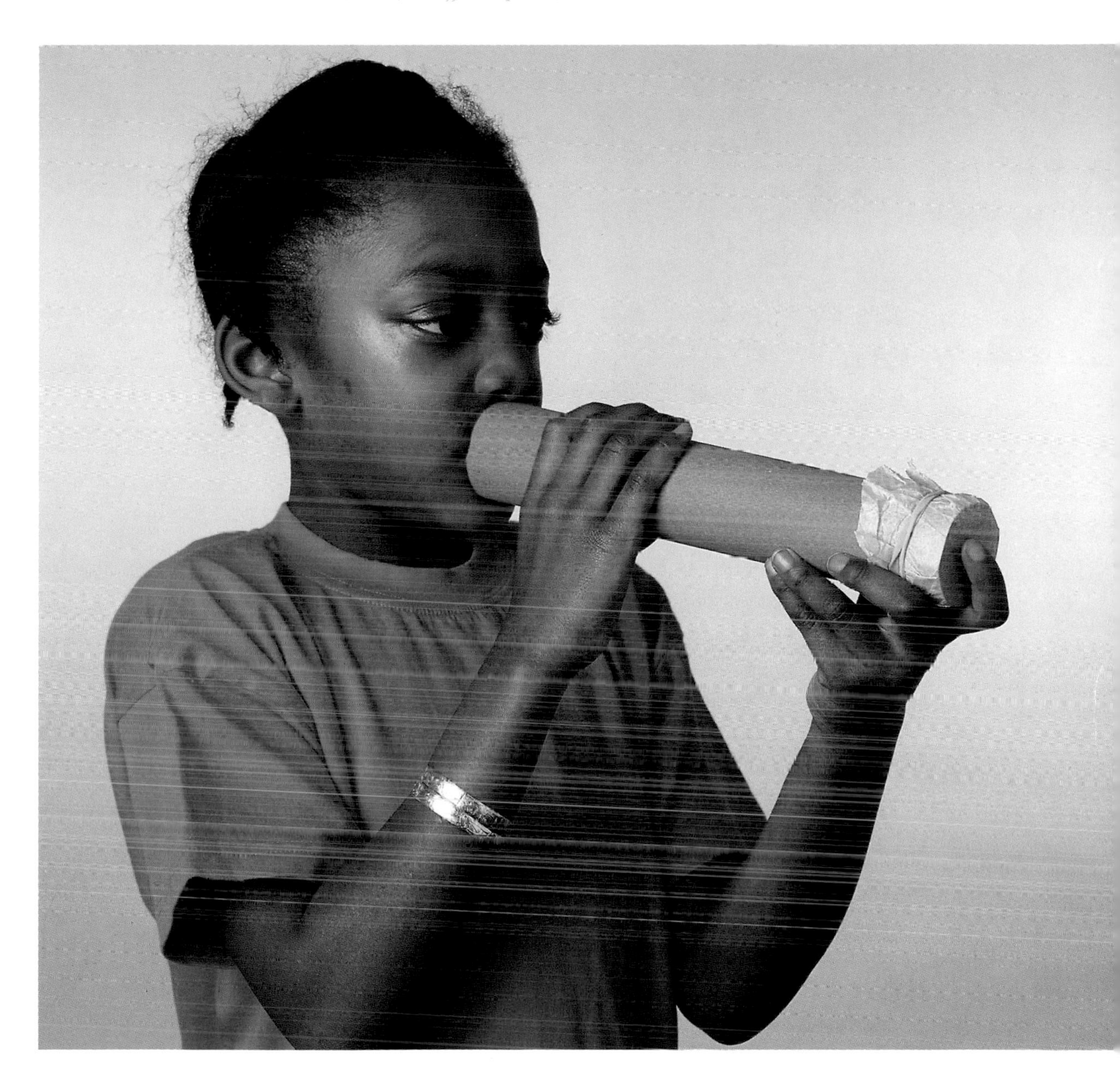

Listen hard

Get ready

✔Pencil ✔Paper

...Get set

Go on a 'listening walk'.
What sounds can you hear indoors?
What sounds can you hear outdoors?
What sounds can you hear
if you sit very still?

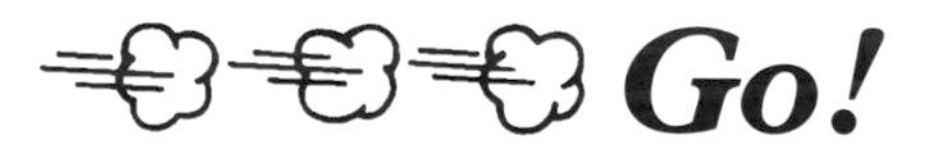

Go!

Make a chart of the sounds you hear.
Write down a word to describe each sound.
Here are some words to help you:
thump, crunch, murmur, tick, rumble,
snap, sizzle, creak, boom, whine, clank.
What other words can you think of?

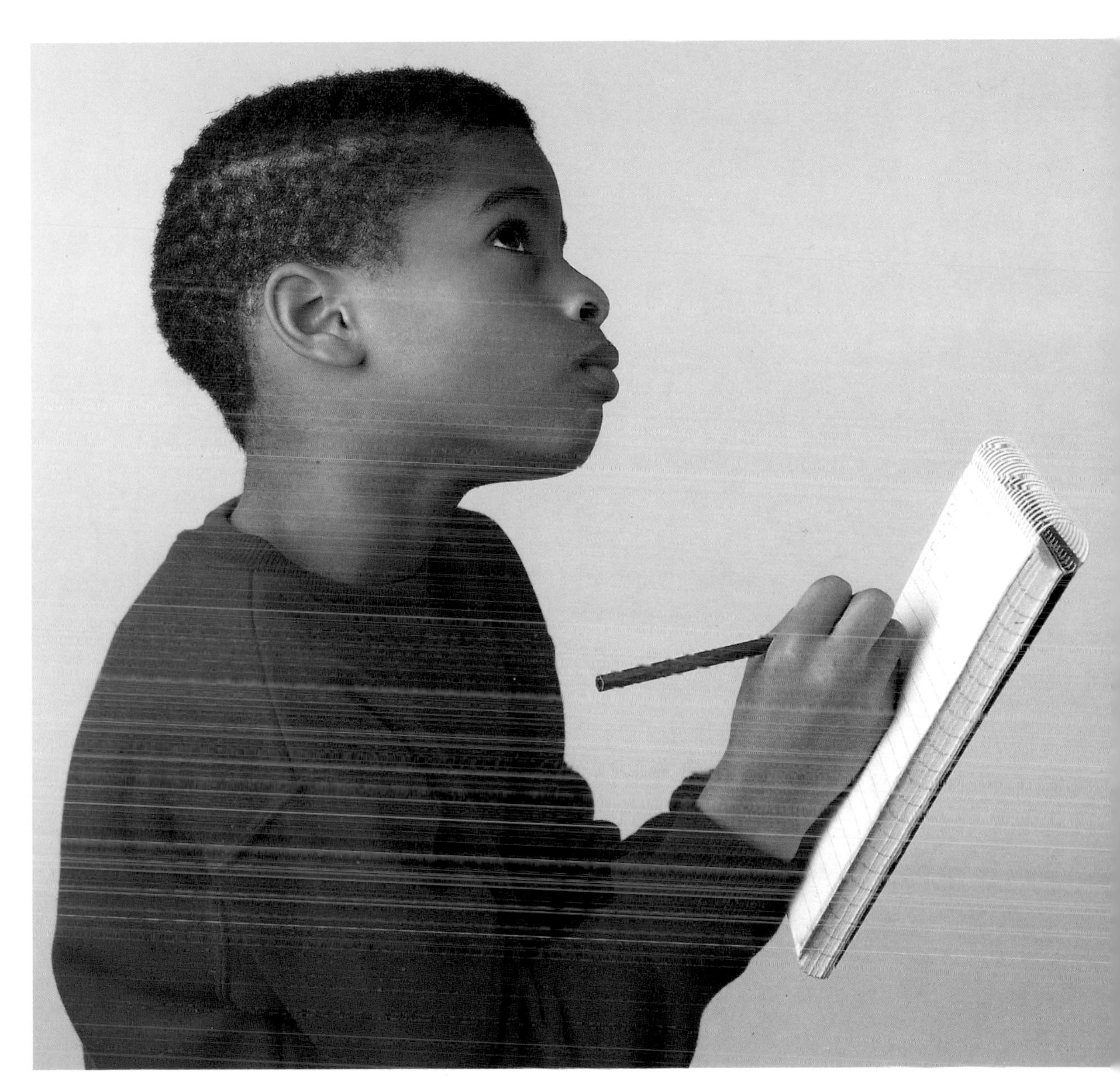

What's that sound?

Get ready

- ✔Jug of water
- ✔Clock
- ✔Paper
- ✔Bowl
- ✔Tin
- ✔Coins

...Get set

Ask two friends to sit with their eyes closed.
Tell one of them to block his ears.
Clap your hands. Stamp your feet.
Tear some paper. Wind up a clock.
Pour water into a bowl.
Shake a tin with coins in it.
Think of some other sounds to try.

 *Go!*

Can your friends both guess
what the sounds are?

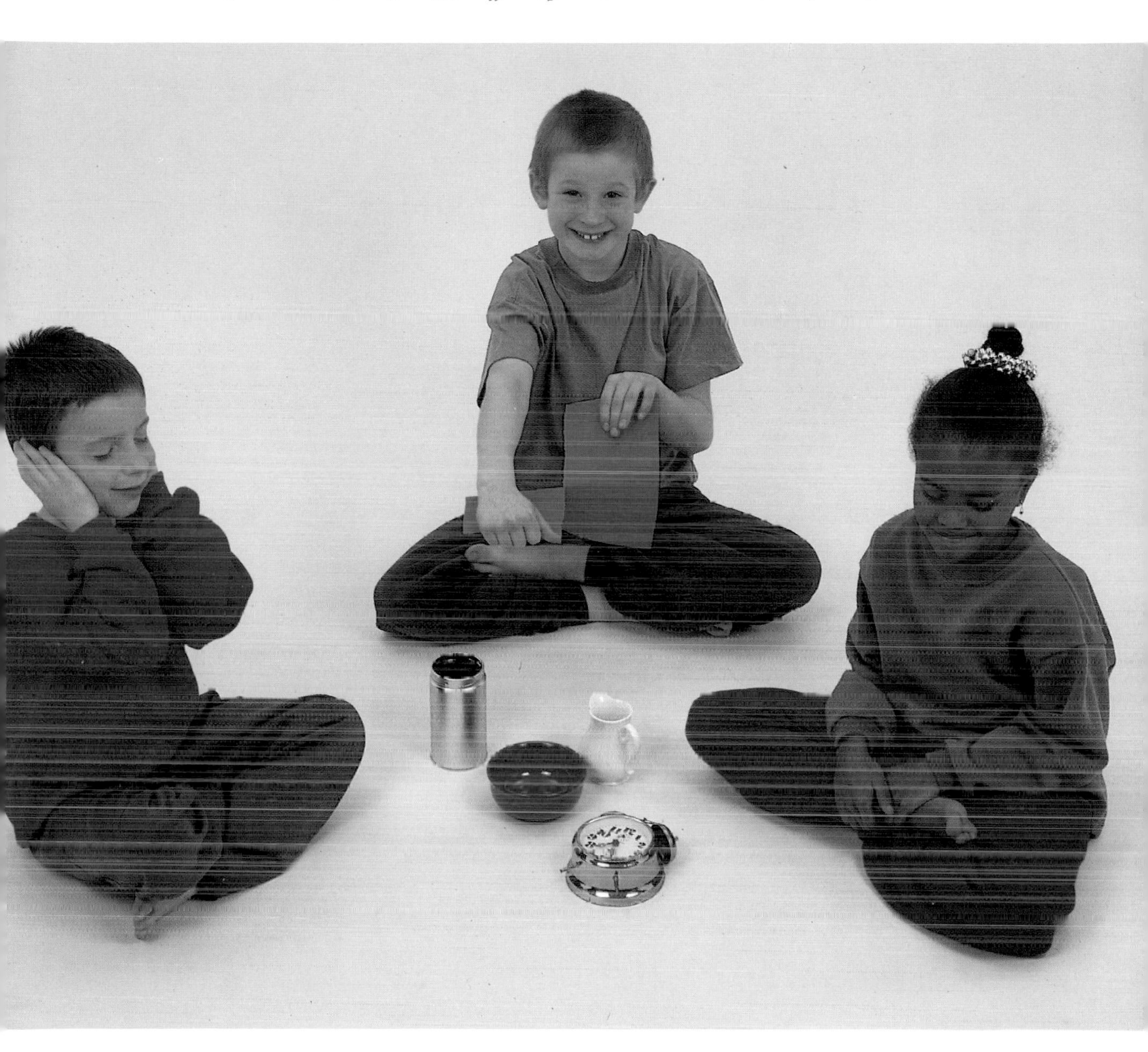

Can you hear this?

Get ready

- ✔Soap bubbles
- ✔Metal tray or lid
- ✔Pin
- ✔Ticking clock

...Get set

Ask a friend to drop a pin on to a metal tray.
Move further away until you cannot hear the sound any more.
Hold a clock near your friend's ear.
Slowly move it further away.
Burst some soap bubbles with a pin.

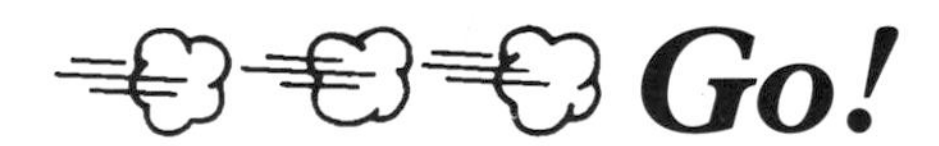

Go!

How far away can you hear a pin drop, a clock tick or a bubble burst?

One ear or two?

Get ready

✔Mug ✔Spoon

...Get set

Sit with your back to a friend.
Ask him to move from right to left,
banging the mug with the spoon.

Go!

Can you always tell which direction
the sound is coming from?
What difference do you notice
if you cover one ear with your hand?

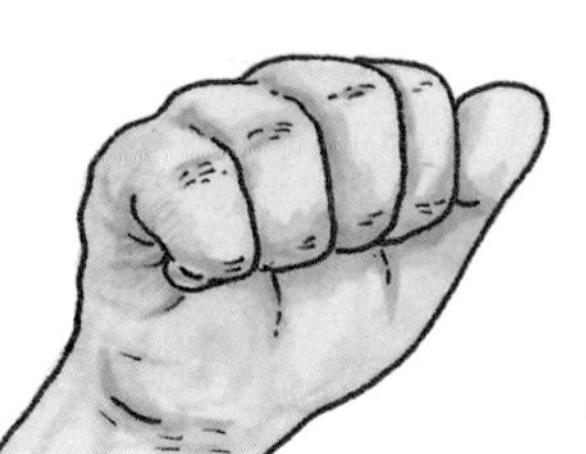

Hear this

Get ready

✔Door

...Get set

Stand on one side of a door.
Ask a friend to stand on the other side
and knock several times.
Now put your ear flat against the door.
Ask your friend to knock again.

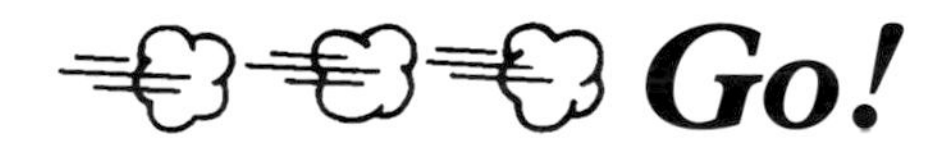

Go!

Can you hear the knocking better
through something solid
or through the air?

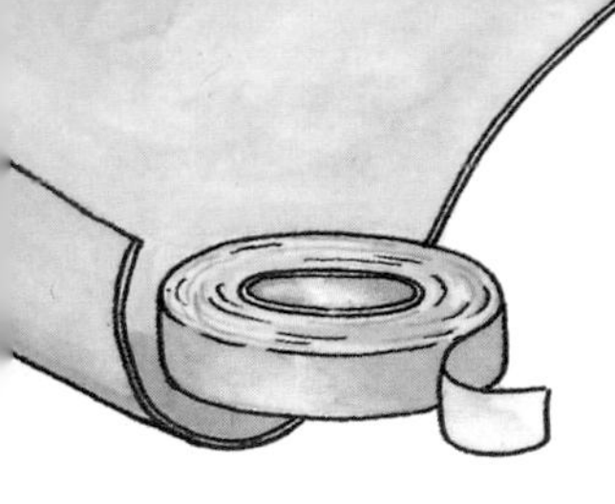

That sounds better

Get ready

✔Sticky tape ✔Sheet of paper

...Get set

Make a megaphone, by rolling
some paper into a cone.
Tape the edges together.
Shout at a friend some distance away
with and without the megaphone.
Now ask your friend to stand behind you.
Shout through the megaphone again.

Go!

When does your shout sound loudest?
When does it sound faintest?
What does the megaphone do to the sound?

Hear, hear

Get ready

✔Whistle ✔Alarm clock ✔Balloon
✔Bell ✔Wooden bricks ✔Pin

...Get set

Hide behind a screen.
Blow the whistle. Clap your hands.
Ring the bell. Bang two bricks together.
Set off the alarm clock.
Burst a balloon with a pin.

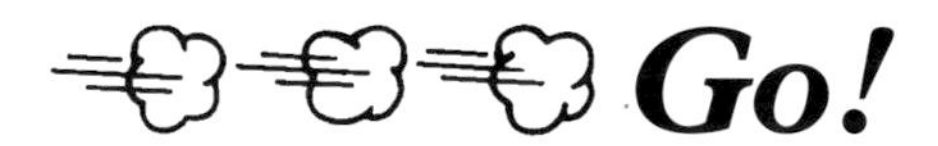

Go!

Can your friend say what each sound is and what information it is giving?
How many sounds can you think of that warn you of danger?

I hear you

Get ready

✔Paints ✔Paintbrush ✔Paper

...Get set

Shriek suddenly. Whisper quietly.
Pretend to cry. Gasp loudly.
Blow a raspberry. Whistle.
Yawn, moan, laugh or whimper.

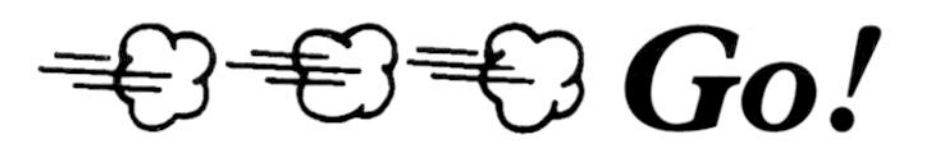

Go!

Can your friends tell how you are feeling?
Make a painting of a sound.
It could be a happy, sad or frightening one.

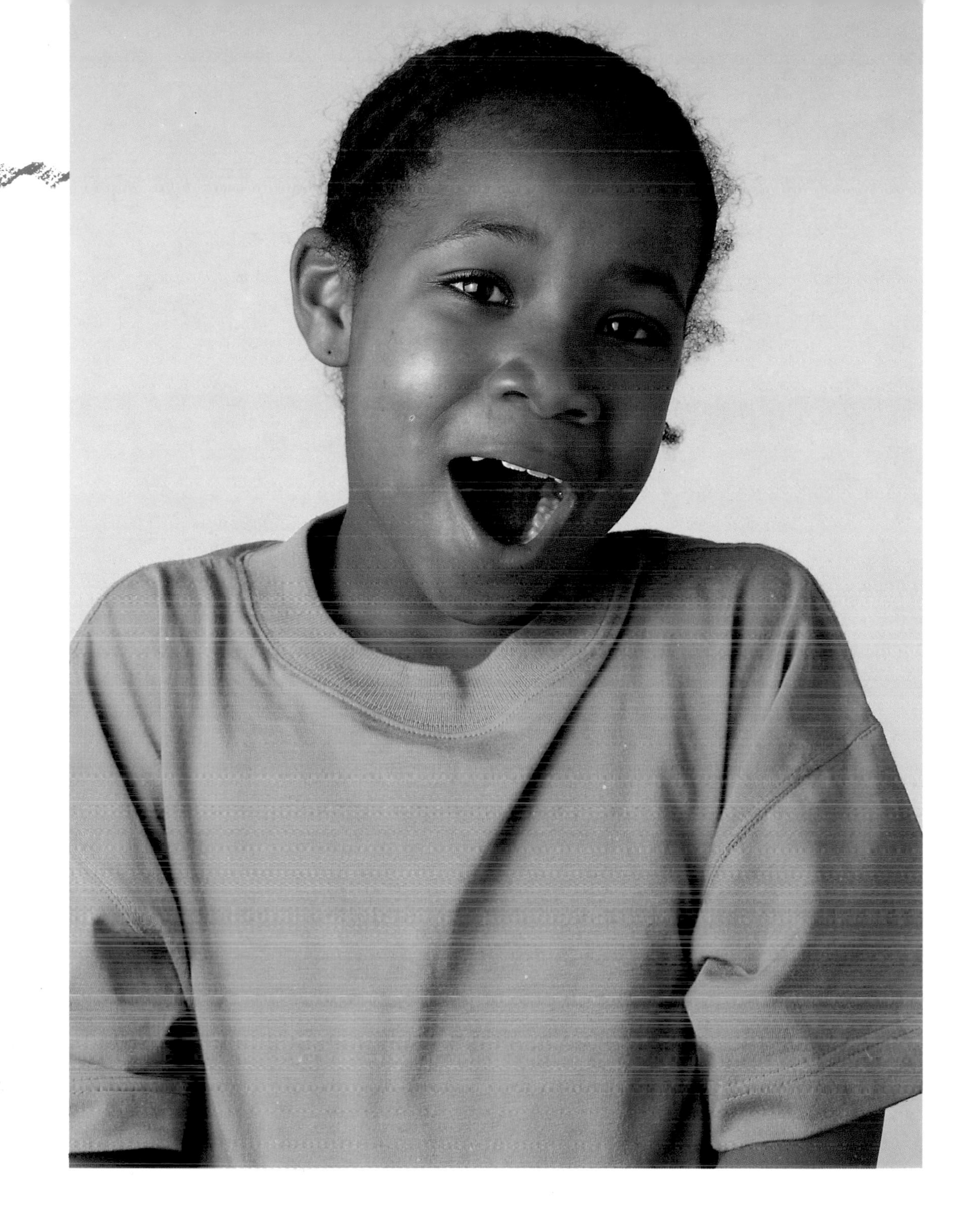

Index

Words that appear in *italics* describe the ideas behind the activities.

Acknowledgments:

The author and publisher would like to thank the pupils of Kenmont Primary School, London, for their participation in the photographs of this book.

Watts Books
96 Leonard Street
London EC2A 4RH

Franklin Watts Australia
14 Mars Road
Lane Cove
NSW 2066

UK ISBN 0 7496 1676 8

10 9 8 7 6 5 4 3 2 1

Series Editor: Pippa Pollard
Editor: Annabel Martin
Design: Ruth Levy
Cover design: Nina Kingsbury
Artwork: Ruth Levy

A CIP catalogue record for this book is available from the British Library

Dewey Decimal Classification 612.8

Printed in Malaysia